spiraling up

How to Create a High Growth, High Value
Professional Services Firm

"Spiraling Up contains business-building insights, based on two years of research, about what makes the-highest-of-high-growth-service-firms tick. The marketing self-assessment in chapter six, alone, is worth the price of the book."

—Mark Levy, Author
Accidental Genius: Using Writing to Generate Your Best Ideas, Insight, and Content

"Spiraling Up is a refreshing book with a clear and creative look at the commonalities and distinctive features among high growth firms. This book doesn't speak down to you it clearly speaks to you through clear writing and phenomenal research and creative graphics. A quick read with great take away nuggets for any professional services firm!"

—Jennifer Abernethy, Author
The Complete Idiot's Guide to Social Media Marketing

"Frederiksen and Taylor tell professional service providers what they don't always want to hear – that they have the means to get the growth they want if they are willing to do the hard thinking and make the hard choices to get it. Great reminder for every firm leader on what it really takes for growth."

—John Doerr, Author
Professional Services Marketing

"Spiraling Up nails it! Any professional services firm whose members embrace and execute these principles will be rewarded richly. Hinge Marketing neatly bundles a whole slew of best practices into a real world formula for success."

—Craig Weeks
Accounting Practice Business Development Blog

"This book provides an exceptional road map of what it takes for Professional Services Firms to be successful in the current chaotic marketplace. The future is now and the research within this publication provides focus for your organization that can position you for high growth in the years ahead and ultimately enhancing the overall value of your company to investors, clients and your employees. We all need a copy of our shelves."

——Ronald D. Worth, CEO
Society for Marketing Professional Services

"Wow. I wish I had this book ten years ago. Spiraling Up has managed to lay down some of the greatest best practices and strategies that have taken us years to develop at our firm. Whether you're just starting, or looking for a kick-start, this is a great read."

—Darryl Ohrt
Brand Flakes for Breakfast Blog

"This book is a must-read for any professional services firm. You'll find fascinating insights into the marketing strategies, operations and attitudes of high growth organizations. What is more these insights are backed up by objective research, proving that a laser focus on your clients' needs and priorities really does get results. And the good news? You can grow without spending vast amounts of money on marketing too."

—Sonja Jefferson
Valuable Content Blog

"Advice of successful CEOs distilled into an easy to understand message, both at the strategic and tactical level. Must read for executives and entrepreneurs wishing to create value in this difficult economic environment in which both the customers and competition can be global."

——Tony Bansal
Internet Executive and Entrepreneur

spiraling up

How to Create a High Growth, High Value
Professional Services Firm

Lee W. Frederiksen, Ph.D.
Aaron E. Taylor

Published by

Hinge Research Institute
www.hingeresearch.com

Special discounts on bulk quantities of this book are available to corporations, professional associations and other organizations. For details contact info@hingemarketing.com or call 703.391.8870.

Spiraling Up:
How to Create a High Growth, High Value Professional Services Firm
Copyright © 2010 by Lee W. Frederiksen and Aaron E. Taylor

Published by Hinge Research Institute
12030 Sunrise Valley Drive, Suite 120
Reston, Virginia 20191

ISBN 978-0-9828819-0-3

Printed in the United States of America

Design by Hinge Marketing.
This book has been designed with 'Hingeitude.'

Visit our website at www.hingemarketing.com

table of contents

acknowledgements

We would like to thank the over 350 executives of
professional services firms who participated in our research.
Without their time and candor, this book would not have
been possible.

Special thanks go to two organizations that participated
with us as valuable research partners—The McLean
Group www.mcleanllc.com and ROI Research on
Investment www.roivision.com.

In addition, several organizations helped provide critical
access to some of the professional services firms we have
studied. Thank you to:

- ○ Society for Marketing Professional Services
  www.smps.org

- ○ Association for Accounting Marketing
  www.accountingmarketing.org

- ○ Harvard Business School Alumni of Northern
  California www.hbsanc.org

- ○ Loudoun County Department of Economic
  Development www.biz.loudoun.gov

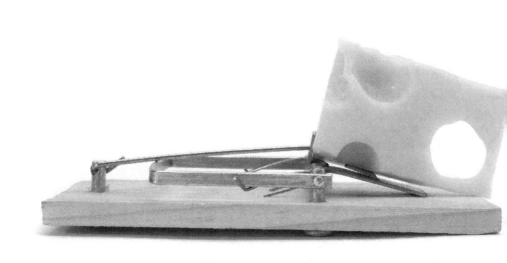

one:

there *must* be a better way

There is a group of highly successful professional services firms that grow nine times faster than their peers and are 50% more profitable. And incredibly, these firms actually spend less than average on marketing and sales.

Not too surprisingly, these firms command premium valuations in the marketplace—sometimes two, five, even ten times revenues! In this book we're going to tell you how they do it, year after year, and how you can too.

Humble Beginnings

At first, we weren't especially interested in high growth firms. We just wanted to build our business. We knew there had to be a better way.

We just wanted to build our business. |

Like you, we run a professional services firm. Our business is helping other professional services firms develop and implement strategy, branding and marketing. So as we began growing our own firm, we did exactly what we recommend to our own clients – start with research. We didn't want to be the shoemaker with barefoot children! In the end, we got a lot more than we bargained for.

As we got deeper into our first set of research, we noticed an interesting pattern among a small group of highly successful firms. Somehow, they were achieving far greater growth than average while spending less on sales and marketing. In our subsequent studies, we continued to see this pattern, and we collected a lot of insights into their success. We were pretty sure we were onto something.

Somehow, they were achieving far greater growth than average while spending less on sales and marketing. |

An Upward Spiral

As one study led to another, we began to understand the dynamics of high growth. For instance, we found that the characteristics contributing to rapid growth also primed these firms for premium valuations. Further, we discovered that those characteristics that acquisition experts valued most were also highly appreciated by clients. And these very satisfied clients drove more referrals and visibility, which in turn fueled further growth.

We were seeing a self-reinforcing pattern that allowed companies to sustain rapid growth and dramatically increase value. We began referring to this happy pattern as spiraling up.

> We were seeing a self-reinforcing pattern that allowed companies to sustain rapid growth and dramatically increase value.

Learning as You Grow

In a way, this book is about a journey. It lays out the discoveries we made over the last several years, more or less in the order that we made them. You will see how our thinking evolved and informed our recommendations.

These discoveries have changed how we run our business. We're living by the results of the research every day. Like you, we're learning and testing our ideas as we grow. We're also sharing them.

This book, and the research studies that came before it, is part of our ongoing commitment to uncover and document the strategies and techniques that contribute to the success of professional services firms.

The insights in this book could help transform your company.

Is This Book for You?

If you are an executive or a marketing director of a professional services firm, the insights in this book could help transform your company. At the very least, our findings should make you rethink your priorities. Some of our findings may challenge your current habits. By the end of Chapter 10 you'll understand how the pieces fit together to generate high growth, exceptional profits and a premium valuation. What will you learn? Here are just a few highlights:

- ○ You can spend your way to growth. But there's a better way.

- ○ Why clients often stop doing business with you even when they're satisfied with your work.

- ○ What counterintuitive strategies and tactics are favored by high growth firms.

- ○ How you can get more referrals from existing clients.

- ○ What the experts look for in high value firms.

So fasten your seatbelts. It's going to get fun!

About the Research

Over three years, Hinge has published four studies that examine different aspects of professional services marketing and management. We interviewed hundreds of CEOs and high-level executives, buyers of professional services, valuation experts, and firms that acquire other firms. We looked specifically at several major professional services industries:

- Accounting & Finance
- Architecture, Engineering & Construction
- Management Consulting & Outsourced Services
- Technology
- Government Contracting

This book is based almost entirely on the findings of our research. To keep it short and readable, we've left out many of the specific data, charts and graphs. If you want more information or supporting evidence, we encourage you to download and read the original research. All of these studies are available for free in the Library section on Hinge's website: www.hingemarketing.com.

Key Takeaways

- ¬ There is a group of professional services firms that grow nine times faster and are 50% more profitable than average.

- ¬ These firms actually spend slightly less than average on sales and marketing and typically receive premium valuations in the marketplace.

- ¬ This book tells you how they do it.

2 ways to grow

We began with a simple question. What's the best way to grow a professional services firm?

We believed we had part of the answer already. After all, we were experienced executives running our own professional services firm. We also had the benefit of insights gained from our daily hands-on experience with professional services clients. But we wanted a more objective, research-based view.

So we began to interview CEOs and managing partners from professional services firms across the country. We had a hunch that marketing spending had a lot to do with growth. "Follow the money" seemed like a reasonable strategy to get at the truth, so we asked these executives how they spend their marketing dollars.

Does spending on marketing drive business growth?

Can You Spend Your Way to Growth?

Many firm executives don't see much correlation between dollars spent on marketing and business growth. Often, they view marketing as a risky investment with an uncertain return. For example, when many professional services executives look at marketing agencies, they can't see past the agencies' obvious self-interest. Agencies talk a big game and charge big bucks, but ultimately they don't have any accountability. As a result, many firms use marketing agencies sparingly.

The flip side, of course, is that professional services firms left to their own devices make haphazard and inconsistent investments in marketing. And because the decision makers usually don't have formal marketing training, these firms rarely have the systems in place to track their progress or learn from experience. It's easy to see why some executives conclude that marketing is an uncertain investment at best.

They don't know any better!

We wanted to banish this confusion once and for all, so we decided to tackle the issue of spending's influence on growth by gathering data from a representative sample of professional services firms. We calculated marketing spending as a percentage of total firm revenue to account for different sizes. Then we divided the firms into three groups:

- Low spenders (the lowest 20%)
- Average spenders (the middle 60%)
- High spenders (the highest 20%)

We learned that average spenders commit about 5% of their revenue to marketing (this number does not include spending on sales). Low spenders were the real misers, ponying up only a half percent of revenue, on average. High spenders, by contrast, invest a healthy 12.0%.

Now, if our theory that marketing spending is related to growth is true, we should see this relationship reflected in our three real-world groups. Sure enough, we found a clear correlation between spending on marketing and revenue growth.

> We found clear correlation between spending on marketing and revenue growth.

Market Spending and Growth

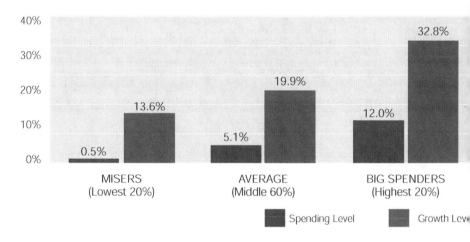

	Spending Level	Growth Level
MISERS (Lowest 20%)	0.5%	13.6%
AVERAGE (Middle 60%)	5.1%	19.9%
BIG SPENDERS (Highest 20%)	12.0%	32.8%

The numbers say it all: the more you spend, the more you grow. This is the clearest indication we've seen anywhere that spending marketing dollars directly influences professional services firm growth.

But not so fast! Put down your checkbook for a moment. Because this is where it gets really interesting.

You can spend your way to growth.
But, there is a better way.

Introducing the High Growth Firm

The takeaway from the data is unmistakable: you can spend your way to growth. But not all spending is the same. It's easy, for instance, to waste marketing dollars. We know this from personal experience. Been there, wasted that. In fact, a lot of firms (maybe most) waste much of their marketing budgets.

But if most companies market themselves inefficiently, a few of them have figured out how to make the most of their marketing dollars. As it turns out, these are the firms that experience the highest rate of growth. And as we were about to learn, they have a different approach to marketing.

When we started our research, it didn't occur to us that we should be looking at high growth firms. In retrospect, of course, it's obvious. But at the time, our discovery came as a bit of a surprise.

> We decided to look more closely at the firms that showed the highest, most consistent rate of growth.

The High Growth Paradox

At some point during our analysis, we decided to look more closely at the firms that showed the highest and most consistent rate of growth. To receive a "high growth" designation, a firm had to demonstrate a minimum growth rate of 20% over each of the past two consecutive years that we studied.

Fewer than a quarter of the companies we interviewed qualified as high growth firms. On average, this group of companies grew 101.2% over the two-year study period. Compare this to average companies, which grew only 18.1%. The high growth firms were growing over 5 times faster than their peers.

Based on our earlier findings, we expected these firms to be spending roughly 5 times more on marketing than their slower growing counterparts. To our surprise, we were wrong.

Instead, we found they were actually spending slightly less than average! These high growth firms were allocating only 4.9% of annual revenue to marketing, compared to the 5.1% level invested by average companies. And of course, that's far below the 12.9% invested by the big spenders.

The fastest growing firms were actually spending less than average on marketing.

So how were these firms achieving extraordinary growth with less-than-average spending? What exactly have they done that's different? The answer comes with its own set of surprises.

Key Takeaways

¬ Increased marketing spending drives growth.

¬ There is an alternative. The highest growth firms actually spend slightly less than average on marketing.

three:

what high growth firms do *differently*

In many ways, high growth firms aren't all that different from average firms. They put a high priority on getting good people, doing quality work and maintaining technical competence. But there are a few things they do differently that set them apart.

And it's these differences that help drive extraordinary growth. In this chapter, we examine some of the key marketing strategies that give high growth firms a competitive advantage.

Market Positioning

Why do clients choose one firm over another? Most firms believe competitive advantage comes from within: their deeper experience, superior expertise, talented staff or client service help them win more contracts. We hear this reasoning from our own clients all the time, and our research shows this sort of thinking is common in the marketplace.

At first blush, the argument makes sense. Who wouldn't want to hire the most experienced and talented firm for their project? But real-world buyers of professional services have grown weary. They've heard every one of these clichés before—almost every firm says more or less the same thing. And clients have stopped listening.

Almost every firm says more or less the same thing. And clients have stopped listening.

High growth firms take a different tack. They choose to talk about issues that hit home with clients. And they back up their words with action. To explain what we mean, let's look at the four most common ways that high growth firms position themselves differently from typical firms:

- They talk about delivering desired outcomes. High growth firms focus on the end result, not their firm's qualifications.

- They are built around the customer. For them, customer service doesn't mean doing what they are told. It's about making the client's life easier. As a result, you don't hear a lot of complaints around the office about clients gumming up the process.

- They are flexible. They understand how much clients value a flexible approach, so many high growth firms feature their flexibility in their marketing.

- They focus on their reputation. This, of course, is a key element in building a professional services brand.

When we share these differences with professional services firm executives we hear a lot of "ah-ha's!" They spot the difference right away—high growth firms focus on their clients' needs and priorities, while average firms are preoccupied with themselves and their expertise.

> High growth firms focus on client needs and priorities, while average firms are preoccupied with themselves and their expertise.

A Matter of Focus

Running a professional services firm can be an all-consuming job. There is always more to do than there is time in the day. We were interested in finding out how top management sets priorities, so we asked executives what they considered most important.

We found that both high growth and average firms put finding and retaining talent at the top of their agendas. This isn't particularly surprising given the central role that people play in professional services firms. And both types of firms try to maintain technical competence, pursue their firm's values and hone areas of special expertise. But beyond this point, things begin to change and high growth firms strike out on a different path.

Average firms, for instance, focus on the economy and competition. This sounds reasonable enough, but it's not where top performers put their time and energy. Top management at high growth firms concentrate instead on marketing and managing growth. Instead of worrying about the market, they focus on growth. Interesting choice.

As we dug deeper, we unearthed other areas of divergence—most notably in the way they go after clients.

High growth firms tended to pursue a well-defined group of target clients.

High growth firms tended to pursue a well-defined group of target clients. Their focus is sharper. Their target is better articulated.

Business Development Priorities

	Target Client Group	Non-Referral Clients
HIGH GROWTH	86.7	77.5
AVERAGE GROWTH	77.0	60.0

(0-100 Scale with 100 most important)

Every professional services company values referral clients. Interestingly, high growth companies place a higher priority on reaching non-referral clients. That means they aggressively go after prospects within a well-defined target group, whether or not they were referred. They don't just take what comes their way. They pursue the prospects they want.

Follow the Money

It's one thing to say something is a priority. It's another matter entirely to put your money where your mouth is. We wondered how high performing companies actually spend their precious marketing dollars. Keep in mind they aren't spending any more than the average performers. Yet those dollars have a far greater impact.

When we compared marketing priorities side by side, the difference was clear. High growth companies generate leads by pushing their message out to a clearly defined target group. They rely on their website to inform and persuade, and they hire outside experts to help them perfect their marketing approach. They also train non-marketing staff to deliver their message and cultivate partners to leverage their efforts.

> High growth companies generate leads by pushing their message out to a clearly defined target group.

Contrast this with average firms. Average firms are much more likely to have no plan. They focus on closing existing prospects, rather than systematically generating new ones. They address revenue problems by hiring additional sales staff and widening their range of products, rather than leveraging their existing resources through training and partnering. Then there is the puzzling issue of thought leadership (see the sidebar for our thoughts on this finding).

Favored Marketing Initiatives

Average Growth Firms	High Growth Firms
Thought Leadership	Increase Awareness
No Plan	Lead Generation
Revise Approach	Website
Close Existing Prospects	Marketing Consultants
Hire Sales People	Train Non-Marketing Staff
Develop New Products	Partnering

Thoughts on Thought Leadership

When we present this research to CEOs, we get a lot of questions about thought leadership. To our surprise, average firms in our study showed a greater affinity for thought leadership than high growth firms. This contradicts conventional wisdom, so we want to explain what we believe is going on.

Upon closer examination, we discovered that what many firms call thought leadership is often so technical and esoteric that it sails over their clients' heads. It's as though they are saying, "Look how smart we are!" You can just picture the glazed-over looks they get. Of course they're smart. They are professionals—everyone assumes they are technically competent.

When high growth firms invest in thought leadership, however, they address issues of greater relevance to their target audiences. These firms want to be known for finding practical answers to clients' common problems. They care less about impressing their peers. So while high growth firms may emphasize thought leadership less, they tend to do it right.

Reaping the Rewards of Referrals

With their emphasis on non-referral business and generating awareness and new leads, we expected high growth firms to have a lower-than-average rate of referrals. As it turns out, that simply isn't true. In this study, high growth firms actually got slightly more referral business than their average peers. Why is that?

We don't have hard data yet to explain this phenomenon, but we have some good hunches. We believe that high growth firms' emphasis on building awareness, generating leads and maintaining a high performing website stimulates referrals. As a firm becomes more visible and top-of-mind, it naturally attracts more referrals.

Referral Business

	% of Referral Business
HIGH GROWTH	59.0%
AVERAGE GROWTH	49.1%

> As a firm becomes more visible and top-of-mind, it naturally attracts more referrals.

We've found that high growth firms tend to have a clearer, easier-to-understand message (see sidebar). Not long ago, for instance, an attorney told us why he had never been able to refer a friend of his—a friend he liked and respected and who worked at what he believed was a very capable firm. The attorney told us sheepishly, "I've asked him three times what his firm does and I still don't understand. I'm embarrassed to ask him again." Need we say more?

> High growth firms tend to have a clearer, easier-to-understand message.

The Elevator Pitch

HIGH GROWTH
72.7%

AVERAGE GROWTH
45.2%

We asked each CEO to give us their brief elevator pitch. We then rated their response on a 5-point scale based on three criteria:
- o Clarity of the firm's capabilities and purpose
- o Clarity of the target market
- o Articulation of the firm's competitive advantage

A rating of 3 or greater is generally acceptable.

Growth Isn't Everything

As we reflected on these results and began to share them with our clients, it became clear that there was a missing dimension. Growth isn't an end in itself. A fast growing firm may be a bubble waiting to burst.

What's really important is the value a firm creates. Which begs the question, "what's the best way to create a high value professional services firm?"

It was time for more research....

Key Takeaways

- High growth firms focus their marketing on their clients' priorities, not their own capabilities.

- High growth firms have a well-defined group of target clients.

- High growth firms focus their limited marketing budgets on their target group.

- A high growth firm's marketing message is clear and easy to understand.

four:
commanding top dollar

If you're reading this book, you probably want to build a firm that has real value. Someday you might even want to sell it. And when you sell you're probably not interested in getting an average price. You'll want to receive top dollar – a premium valuation. What will it take?

That's the question we posed in our next research study, which focused on premium valuations. In any industry, certain firms command much higher multiples than their peers. Why is that? What are they doing differently?

For answers, we turned to two groups that have an insider's perspective on company value:

Buyers of professional services firms. Buyers are often large companies—sometimes publicly held, sometimes private—that acquire compatible firms to grow their business. In other cases, these buyers are private equity firms.

Independent business valuation experts. These are professionals who have deep experience valuing professional services firms. It's what they do every day.

What Drives Premium Valuation?

We asked our study participants to recall a specific instance when they gave a professional services firm a premium valuation. We wanted to build an understanding based on real experience, not hypotheticals.

Our participants were able to cite plenty of examples. Some of the premiums they reported assigning to businesses were eye-popping. Our personal favorite is ten times revenue.

Some Premium Valuations

Valuing a professional services firm is different than valuing other types of businesses. Service firms usually don't have a lot of hard assets, such as real estate or inventory. And cash and receivables are only modest factors. In general, the buyer of a professional services firm is interested in only one thing: the expectation of future revenue.

> Acquirers are purchasing the expectation of future revenue.

What characteristics, we wondered, make buyers swoon and valuation experts add zeros to their appraisals? What, exactly, brightens the expectation of future revenue? We identified 33 separate factors that could drive value. These included financial considerations (such as profitability and growth rate), employee characteristics, brand and marketing, client characteristics, management team qualifications and technology.

Let's look at the top five value drivers, starting at the bottom and working our way up.

Value Driver 5: Quality of Management Team

Don't get us wrong, the senior management team can make a big difference. But it may disappoint CEOs or managing partners to learn that top management is rarely the most critical factor in a firm's valuation. Acquirers assume that the leadership will take their fat payout and head for Tahiti. Nor do the front line employees matter most. If front line personnel were unusually skilled, they would probably be difficult to recruit and retain—limiting the expectation of future revenue. Even highly regarded "rainmakers" get relatively little respect from valuation experts. Why? If clients are loyal to a rainmaker instead of the firm (as is often the case), they will leave when the rainmaker decides to find another home.

Instead, the real hero is the much maligned, rarely appreciated middle management. These are the men and women who make a firm run day in and day out. They are the key to maximizing value.

> The real hero is the much maligned, rarely appreciated middle management.

Value Driver 4: Quality of Earnings

It's not too surprising that earnings make the top 5 list. But here's something that might raise an eyebrow: it's the quality, not the size, of earnings that matters most.

Most of us expect firms with higher earnings to be more valuable. And to a certain extent that's true. In general, a high profit margin is better than a low one.

But as anyone who has run a professional services firm knows, there are a lot of ways to artificially boost the bottom line in the short term, whether it's deferring hardware upgrades, understaffing critical functions or failing to properly account for questionable receivables.

> Savvy buyers understand that artificially inflated earnings are not sustainable.

Savvy buyers understand that artificially inflated earnings are not sustainable. To achieve a substantial bottom line over time, a firm must generate high quality earnings. No fancy footwork allowed.

Value Driver 3: Existing Client Contracts

Nothing quite locks in future revenue like a long-term contract with a financially sound client. It's a good way to remove uncertainty from future revenue projections.

But client contracts represent more than just projectable revenue. If clients are willing to enter into multi-year contracts, two other things must be true. First, the client expects they will have an ongoing need. Second, they believe the firm will be able to meet that need better than anyone else. If a firm's clients don't believe these two things, the firm won't accumulate long-term contracts. But if the conditions are met, the contracts—and associated revenue—are more likely to follow.

Nothing quite locks in future revenue like a long-term contract with a financially sound client.

Value Driver 2: Projected Growth Rate

It's pretty easy to see how a firm's projected growth rate helps drive valuation. That assumes, of course, the projection is believable.

How do you make projections believable? The best way is to base them on a proven, scalable process. Let's look at a hypothetical example.

Suppose you know from past experience that by spending $200,000 on a direct mail campaign to a random sample of your target audience you can reliably produce $4,000,000 of profitable business. Now suppose you can prove that your target audience is large enough that you could ramp up that marketing program to $2,000,000 (in this case, 10 times your sample size). You could project with reasonable certainty that you could generate $40,000,000 in sales from that effort. Voilá! You've projected a marketing program that is both proven and scalable.

The most believable projections are based on a proven, scalable process.

By contrast, if you try to create a projection based on the personal networking and business development efforts of top management or a well-connected rainmaker, you're going to have a much tougher time making your case to a potential buyer. Can you systematically demonstrate that their development activities result in new business? Is the model easily scalable? If you answer "no" to either of these questions, then the basis for your projected growth rate is suspect.

Value Driver 1: Strength of Existing Client Relationships

When it comes to commanding a premium valuation, nothing is more important than the strength of your client relationships. By "client relationship," we aren't talking about how often you golf or vacation together. While these activities may drive some sales, personal relationships can't be transferred to a new owner, nor are they scalable. Consequently they add very little real value to your firm.

In fact, the most valuable client relationships are based on ongoing business relationships between firms. They have very little to do with personal chemistry. Instead, they are relationships that provide proven value to clients—value that both sides acknowledge and can be documented. Put another way, a firm should have a strong "brand" within their clients' world.

Let's look at an example. Suppose that after hiring your firm a client is able to perform a critical function for half the cost of doing it themselves. And suppose the results your firm created give the client a measurable advantage in the marketplace. This quantifiable value is the basis of a strong and stable client relationship and is much more important than personal chemistry alone.

Nothing is more important than the strength of your client relationships.

No Fancy Furniture Required

Physical assets didn't make our list, but we thought they were worth a mention since they can usually be converted into hard cash. According to our experts, physical assets were the least important factor for driving a premium valuation. So much for that fancy new office furniture!

Building a High Value Firm

Where do you begin building a firm that embodies these key value drivers? When we asked our research participants this question, we got the same two answers: grow strategically and differentiate your firm. These two practices will provide a solid platform for building a premium value.

All growth is not created equal. |

Grow Strategically

All growth is not created equal—some types are better than others. One of our experts put it succinctly: "Avoid growth without strategy." Growth for growth's sake leaves valuation experts cold.

So what is strategic growth? Simply stated, it's growth that has a clear focus and builds on an easy-to-understand strategy. To grow strategically you need to **1)** define your target audience clearly (and usually this means having a narrow focus); **2)** make sure your service delivers superior value; and **3)** be confident that demand for your services will grow over time.

What isn't strategic? You see it everywhere: offering a wide-ranging set of generalized services to a broad audience—being everything to everyone. Can you build a firm on that foundation? Sure, it happens all the time. Will it command a premium valuation? Not likely.

Focus on a Strong Differentiator

It's not easy to find a differentiator that truly sets a professional services firm apart in the marketplace. If you can establish one, it can give you a real competitive advantage. Unfortunately most firms never find a compelling differentiator.

Professional services firms that try to differentiate themselves typically fall into one of two traps:

1. **They fail to differentiate themselves.** Most firms say more or less the same thing as their competitors. Their website and marketing materials make them look like their competitors. They believe they have the best people, are more dedicated to their clients and offer superior service. To a potential client, however, it all sounds drearily familiar.

Unless you can point to some concrete factor that makes you different, you aren't. If you can't say or do something that your competitors are not, you won't be perceived as different.

2. **They differentiate themselves in a way that doesn't resonate with clients.** Many firms claim to have superior technical expertise in specific areas. Because they have little to do with the problem at hand, these differences in competence or technology are lost on most potential clients. They simply don't care.

While it may be important to you, superior technical competence is often either irrelevant to solving a client's problem or not fully appreciated. If your potential client can't see it or doesn't value it, your differentiator doesn't exist.

> If your potential client can't see it or doesn't value it, your differentiator doesn't exist.

Strong differentiators are out there. If competitors take six months to complete a project and you do it in one month, that's a differentiator. If your industry sells services by the hour and you get paid based on the outcome, that's a differentiator. If your competitors serve many industries and you specialize in a single vertical, that's a differentiator. But if your competitors have great people and you have great people, too—you've got some work to do. (For more on differentiation, see the sidebar on page 86.)

A Pattern Emerges

Now things were getting interesting. With two research studies behind us, we were beginning to see a distinct pattern. That pattern looked an awful lot like a bull's eye with the client at its center. It was pretty clear that the client relationship is critical to achieving a premium valuation—and building a high growth firm.

Any firm would agree that solving the client's key problems is important. Yet most firms are not high performers. What are they missing that high growth, high value firms understand? What exactly do clients want? And how do you get them to choose your firm, anyway?

Once again, we were going to find out.

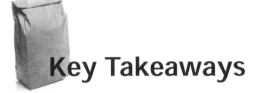

Key Takeaways

- ¬ The value of a firm is based on the expectation of future revenue.

- ¬ Middle management is critical to delivering superior results.

- ¬ High quality, projectable revenue adds value.

- ¬ The client relationship is at the center of a premium valuation.

- ¬ Growth that is strategic and protected by a clear and strong competitive advantage is likely to be of most value.

five:

how and why clients buy

Our next step was pretty clear. It was time to look at what goes on between the client's ears.

In our valuation study, introduced in Chapter 4, we determined that the client relationship was central to achieving a premium valuation. In addition, we learned that high growth performance was linked to a firm's ability to focus on a narrow group of target clients.

These insights, of course, raised more questions. How do clients select firms? Why do some relationships grow and others wither? When and why do clients make referrals? To get some answers, we conducted another series of in-depth interviews—this time with buyers of professional services.

Meet Your Competition

If you're like most firms, you've got a bead on your competition. You probably track which firms beat you in competitive bid situations. You may visit competitors' websites, read their press releases and save their marketing materials. You might even interview their former employees to gain insight into their business. And you may conduct broad searches to identify potential competitors, carefully evaluating their competencies and offerings.

There's only one small problem... your potential clients don't see the world the way you do. It's like clients are from Venus and firms are from Mars. They have entirely different perspectives.

80 percent of your competitors aren't even on your radar.

We invited a group of firms to list their competitors. Then we called up their clients and asked them to identify other companies they believed offer the same service. What we found was a real eye-opener. In most cases, there was less than 20% overlap in the two lists. This means that over 80 percent of your competitors aren't even on your radar! How can this be?

Identifying the Competition

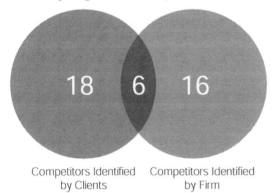

| Competitors Identified
by Clients | Competitors Identified
by Firm |

When we went back to the firms and showed them the clients' lists of competitors, we heard a lot of: "I've never heard of them," and "They don't do that" or "Why would the client see them as a competitor? They're not competent to do that."

Let's face it, most firms have two things working against them. On the one hand, they know too much. Firms dismiss many competitors because they know (or think they know) those companies can't match their expertise. On the other hand, they aren't exposed to the wide range of alternative market solutions that clients are considering. Many firms will draw fine technical distinctions that their prospective clients simply can't see or don't understand.

> Many firms will draw fine technical distinctions that their prospective clients simply can't see or don't understand.

For example, a firm knows that company X doesn't have the internal resources to properly solve a client's problem. So they rule them out as a competitive threat. The client sees a different reality. Both firms use similar words to describe themselves and both have impressive credentials and references. As a result, the potential client assumes both companies are equally qualified to solve their problem. They don't necessarily understand what resources are required to get the job done.

If left to their own devices, buyers will identify a competitive landscape that is very different from the one you inhabit. It's in a firm's best interest to stand out as a superior alternative.

Before a firm can stand out, however, it needs to understand how clients would like to be marketed to.

How to Improve Your Marketing

Most buyers of services are flooded with marketing messages. Here are just a few common ways professional services market to prospective clients:*

- ○ Cold calls

- ○ Email

- ○ Networking

- ○ Direct mail

* Listed in descending order of frequency, based on our research findings.

- Personal visits

- Conferences

- Ads in trade pubs

But which approaches generate the most positive responses from buyers?

To find out, we asked our survey participants how firms could improve their marketing. The results were striking. Their list of suggestions could be a blueprint for how to win their business: "Offer me a personalized understanding of my situation with no high pressure sales calls." "When you talk with me, present a detailed solution to my problem and relevant case studies to back it up." "Meet with me personally and show me that you want our business."

Buyers just want you to start a dialog about solving their problems. They aren't interested in another sales pitch. "I don't want to be sold to," explained one of our respondents. "Have a good understanding of my situation, then sit down with me and lay out a detailed solution. Show me how it has worked before."

> Buyers want what buyers want, not what's easiest for you.

We know it's not fair or logical. How can you possibly offer a detailed understanding of a buyer's situation before you even know their situation? But buyers want what buyers want, not what's easiest for you. As you will see below, some firms are better positioned to handle this situation.

The Specialist's Advantage

Most client problems aren't unique. Any firm with relatively deep experience in a buyer's industry has probably dealt with a similar situation before. That's why specialists have a real advantage. In many situations, they can produce detailed case studies and present well thought-out solutions at the drop of a hat—because they've seen it all before. Non-specialists, on the other hand, have to dig deep and pull out their closest comparable solution. If all goes well, it might be enough to gain the buyer's confidence, but it's a much tougher sell.

High growth firms' narrow focus on a well-defined target group gives them a competitive advantage over their less focused peers.

The high growth firms we discussed earlier can market so efficiently in part because their narrow focus on a well-defined target group gives them a competitive advantage over their less focused peers.

That built-in advantage is important to building a competitive edge. Now, let's look more closely at the selection process as it plays out in the real world.

Pick Me! Pick Me!

What are potential clients looking for in a firm? When we asked buyers of professional services to identify the most meaningful criteria for selecting a firm, no single answer stood out above the rest. Five criteria, however, accounted for about three quarters of their responses: expertise/technical skill, quality of the project team, firm experience, past industry/service experience and firm reputation. Interestingly, price was cited only 4.2% of the time.

Now, let's look at the flip side: what buyers were trying to avoid when selecting a firm. Their answers provide a deeper understanding into the qualities they value most in a firm.

Above all, buyers want to avoid poor results and failing to solve their problem. This makes a lot of sense. Three of the five top selection criteria address avoiding failure: expertise, experience and industry knowledge. Let's be careful, though. This doesn't

mean the firm with the greatest technical experience will get the job. As we noted earlier, many clients are not equipped to evaluate technical expertise.

The second most important issue when selecting a firm was the quality of the project team. We could hear the pain in their voices as buyers told us stories of arrogance, rigidity or self-centeredness. "Our project manager was more concerned with keeping the project on schedule and meeting her milestones than she was with giving us what we needed. It was very frustrating," recalled one respondent.

The third most cited issue was high fees and cost overruns. When a buyer is confident that a single firm can overcome their problems, price becomes less of an issue. When several firms are all qualified to meet their objectives, then cost becomes a factor. Firms that aren't qualified to solve their problem won't make the cut, no matter how low their fees.

If you can't convince prospective clients that you can solve their problem, nothing else matters.

What Do Clients Really Want?

So how do we sum up what clients really want? After carefully reviewing all the results of our research, we concluded that buyers are looking for answers to just three fundamental questions:

1. Can you fix my problem?

The bulk of the selection criteria throughout the process are aimed at answering this question. Do you understand my situation? Have you solved a similar problem before? Do you have the skills to do the job? This is the threshold issue. If you can't convince prospective clients that you can solve their problem, nothing else matters. Keep in mind that their real problem may not be the one that's on the RFP. They may not even fully understand what the real problem is. But you have to convince them that you can and will solve it. This often involves reframing the issue or reading between the lines.

> Prospective clients want to know how difficult, painful, or expensive the process will be.

2. Will you make my life easier?

A client's next biggest concern is how difficult, painful or expensive the process will be. Issues include such things as cost, availability, responsiveness and customer service. If two competing firms appear equally equipped to solve the problem, the selection will be made at this level.

> Relationships matter. But they don't trump a firm's ability to meet the first two criteria.

3. Do I enjoy you as a person?

Relationships matter. But they don't trump a firm's ability to meet the first two criteria. If a buyer likes you, they may give you preference, but they're not going to hire you if they don't believe you can solve their problem. Nor are they likely to hire you if your price is significantly higher or you come across as inflexible or arrogant. On the other hand, if a buyer believes you grasp their problem and can solve it—and if you are competitively priced and easy to work with—you will be tough to beat.

It's your job make sure your prospective clients can answer "yes" to these three questions as early in the process as possible. That will usually get you in the door. But what happens next? Let's find out.

Key Takeaways

¬ Firms don't necessarily know who their real-world competitors are.

¬ Buyers want you to understand their specific situation and show that you know how to improve it.

¬ The highest priority is to convince buyers that you can solve their problem.

¬ Considerations such as service, price and relationship are important only if buyers believe you are able to deliver results.

SIX:

expanding client relationships

Has this ever happened to you? A client seems perfectly content with your firm. More than once, they've told you how happy they were with your services and how they want to work with you again in the future.

Then one day, you look up and they've hired one of your competitors to provide a service that your firm can do with its eyes closed. And you weren't even asked for a bid. Puzzled, you think back. You remember telling the client early-on in the engagement about that very service—it's even on your website, for Pete's sake! So what gives?

Well, get prepared. The problem is even worse than you feared.

"Oh.... You Do That?"

There is a very good chance your client would have given that project to you outright ... if they'd just known you offered it. (We'll take a brief pause while you bang your head against the desk.)

Yep, you told them about that service offering—but that was a while ago. And if they are like most clients, they haven't even glanced at your website since they first hired you.

You see, the client has pegged your firm for one thing—the service they hired you for. They won't think about you in any other way. When a new need arose in a different area, they started a fresh search.

If this has happened to you, you're in good company— it's all too common. In fact, we've faced it, ourselves. As a result, we wanted to get some insight into the problem.

First, we asked clients if they believed they were aware of all the services their current firm provided. Almost two thirds of clients admitted they weren't aware.

(When we share this result with seasoned executives most tell us that even many clients who "think they know" are probably wrong.)

Next, we asked the clients if they could think of any additional services they wished their current provider would offer. Almost three quarters offered up new services they wanted from their current provider.

> Over 85% of the time firms already offered what the client wanted – only the client didn't know it!

We then went back to the providers to find out if any of those requested services were in their current portfolio. Guess what? Over 85% of the time they already offered what the client wanted – only the client didn't know it!

As many of us have learned the hard way, when clients don't know you offer a specific service, they have an exasperating tendency to find it somewhere else. So what's the solution? Well, it starts by gaining an appreciation of how clients want to hear about new services.

Offering New Services

We asked clients how they wanted to be notified about new service offerings. A small number preferred that service firms stick to a structured procurement process. For the most part, these are the procurement departments of government agencies or large corporations. Others said they wanted firms to use various marketing vehicles to reach them, such as a newsletter or mailing.

But the vast majority—three quarters of our sample— asked for a more personal approach. Clients want firms to discuss their business challenges and offer proven solutions. As one person put it, "Have a senior person sit down with me and discuss my business situation. If there is a way they can help me, make a recommendation."

Whose Job Is It?

When you are trying to expand a client relationship, keep this in mind: it's not your client's responsibility to figure out how your firm can help. That's your job.

> It's not your client's responsibility to figure out how your firm can help. That's your job.

Some firms task their project managers with finding new opportunities as they interact with clients. But there are serious limitations to this approach. Project managers are usually focused on getting current projects completed on time, on budget and within scope—not to mention keeping the client happy. The last thing they have time to think about is business development. When operational imperatives collide with business development, operations always win.

When operational imperatives collide with business development, operations always win.

As it turns out, clients aren't inclined to discuss their needs with project managers, anyway. They are far more likely to open up to a providing firm's upper management. When an upper-level executive—with the experience to make an accurate diagnosis and present a credible solution—takes the time to sit down with a client, get to know them and understand their situation, the client will usually be willing, even eager, to discussing other challenges they face.

From time to time, we hear executives complain that they have trouble getting appointments with clients. In most cases, they simply aren't communicating their value or benefits when they call. Few clients want to be sold to. Almost everyone, however, wants their key problems solved. If you are seen as providing that value, you'll get the appointment.

Client Loyalty

Let's shift gears for a moment and address another thorny issue: why do clients leave? How can you command their loyalty?

When we asked clients why they stuck with their current firm, over two thirds of them reported they did so because the firm delivers on its promises. It addresses their challenges. "They communicate that the firm knows my business, knows my problems, and knows how to solve my problems," said one participant. That pretty much says it all.

Okay, that's why they stay. But why do they go? According to our research, clients shed their service providers for one of two reasons: **1)** the firm didn't deliver on its promise; or **2)** the client couldn't identify a need that the firm could meet. About 60% of the cases fall into the second category—so that represents a huge missed opportunity. If in fact most clients don't know all the services their firms offer, then many satisfied clients are moving on because they don't believe their current providers can help them further.

Satisfied clients will move on because they don't believe there is any more you can do to help them.

Getting Referral Business

Most firms cherish referral business. Referred clients costs little or nothing to cultivate, close more quickly and are usually easier to manage. We wanted to better understand the dynamics behind the referral process so that we—and our professional services clients—could recreate it.

Making a Referral

Rating	Percentage	Already Referred
9-10	66.9%	79.0%
7-8	24.2%	52.9%
6 or Less	8.9%	0.0%

We started by assessing the likelihood of making a referral using the 0-10 scale developed by Reicheld and others.* We learned that about two thirds of clients were very happy; in fact, almost 80% of these clients had made referrals already. Another quarter was on the fence, with ratings of 7 or 8. Just over half of this group had made referrals. The remaining clients (under 9%) were negative about the firm, and none had made referrals.

> 60% of referrals are made in response to a request for a recommendation.

Not All Referrals Are Equal

We uncovered two types of referrals:

- Most referrals (about 60%) are given in response to a request. In other words, someone asked for a recommendation.

* Reicheld, Fred. *The Ultimate Question: Driving Good Profits and True Growth*. Boston: Harvard Business Press, 2006.

○ The rest are more proactive. For example, a business problem comes up in conversation and somebody recommends a firm to address the issue.

The latter type of referral is the best. These clients are so enthusiastic about the firm that they refer it without prompting. Think of them as evangelists.

When we asked why people didn't refer, slightly less than three quarters of our respondents told us that nobody had asked. Outside of the evangelists, most people don't go out of their way to make a referral. But when asked, they'll gladly make one.

So how do you encourage more referrals? First, figure out which of your clients are making proactive referrals. You can do this by tracking referral sources. Or you can assess it directly by asking clients the "likelihood to refer" question. Then be sure to give your referring clients the support they need to continue this behavior.

Support can take a variety of forms. For many referrers, a small gift or verbal thanks is all it takes. A few like to have your firm's marketing materials or business cards on hand. If in doubt, just ask them what they need. And don't forget to lavish them with your appreciation.

You'll want to encourage prospects to reach out to those clients who dole out referrals on request. These clients usually make excellent references. Feature them in case studies or articles to stimulate inquiries. The vast majority of the time, you'll get a favorable response.

The Client Has Spoken

Clients have told us what they want. First, they want their problem solved. This means your initial task is to identify a client's problem. Be careful. Don't become order takers. More often than not, the problem a client wants to fix is just the tip of the iceberg, and you may need to look deeper to find the real issue. That's how you deliver real value.

Second, they want you to make their lives easier. Anticipate needs. Make your firm easy to deal with. Clients want you to take care of the details. Keep them apprised of your progress on an ongoing basis—don't keep them guessing. Make pricing fair and transparent. Do what you say you will do.

One More Step

The pieces were fitting together: High growth and high value are two sides of the same coin, both revolving around clients and the value a firm brings to them.

Two years of research and three published studies later, we nearly had the answers we needed. But we had a few gaps to fill first. How do you actually go about building a high growth, high value firm? What strategies work best? How do you differentiate your firm? How do you go about understanding what clients want? We needed one more study to understand how to get the upward spiral started.

Key Takeaways

- Clients are unaware of the services you provide and how you could help them.

- Most clients prefer that you identify problem areas and suggest solutions.

- Clients most often stop doing business with a firm not because they are dissatisfied but because they no longer have an identified need that they believe their current firm can address.

- The majority of referrals are made in response to a specific request for a recommendation.

seven:
marketing the high growth way

By this point, we had come almost full circle. When we started out, we wanted to uncover proven methods to grow a professional services firm. Along the way, we stumbled upon a group of firms that were growing exceptionally fast without spending a lot of marketing money.

We then looked at firms that command premium valuations and found that they shared many things in common with high growth firms—especially a laser focus on the client. This discovery led us to explore the needs of their clients: buyers of professional services.

Next, it was time to turn the magnifying glass on the object of our quest, high growth firms themselves. How did they do it? Were they really as good as they seemed? Can their results be replicated?

A Simple Plan

Our plan was simple. We would identify high growth, high value firms and compare them to a group of average growth firms from the same industries. We would look systematically at their strategies, their approach to clients and how they invested their business dollars. We would also dig deeper into their financial performance to see if they were as profitable as their peers.

To pull this off we enlisted the help of two research partners. The McLean Group, a national investment banker specializing in mid-market companies, helped us locate a pool of high growth, high value firms. A second partner, ROI Research on Investment, identified a control group of average growth firms and helped us conduct interviews with CEOs.

Our plan wasn't bad. But our timing was, well, interesting.

> We were studying high growth and high value performance during the worst financial crisis since the Great Depression

Crisis Time

Our research spanned the years 2008 and 2009. That means we were studying high growth and high value performance during the worst financial crisis since the Great Depression. Sounds kind of ill advised, doesn't it?

In fact, it may have been inspired timing. Was there ever a better laboratory to understand the factors that deliver high growth and high value? Extreme economic pressures only magnified the differences between high and average performance. In retrospect, they were interesting times indeed.

Spending and Growth: Revisited

One unanswered question in our minds was the relationship between spending and growth. In our first study we had looked at marketing spending, but we had neglected the cost of selling. This time we were careful to look at all business development spending, including marketing and sales costs. What we found mirrored our marketing-only data, with a single exception: at the highest spending level, firms seemed to lose some "leverage." They reached a plateau where they were spending as much on business development as they were bringing in from new business. Perhaps the decreased level of absolute demand driving the economic crisis limited their ability to "buy" growth.

Market Spending and Growth

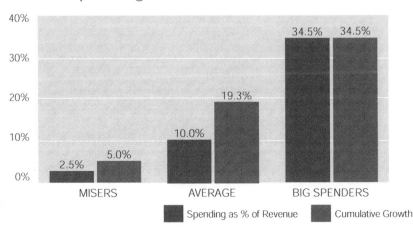

MISERS — 2.5% / 5.0%
AVERAGE — 10.0% / 19.3%
BIG SPENDERS — 34.5% / 34.5%

Spending as % of Revenue   Cumulative Growth

High Growth Firms

High growth firms were able to distance themselves from average growth firms by a wide margin. Over the two years of this study, they sustained an average growth of 90.1% compared to the 10% growth experienced by average firms. That's a nine-fold performance difference.

The High Growth group found a way to grow faster without spending more than average.

Once again, the high growth group found a way to grow faster without spending more than average. Their total spending on business development was slightly less than spending at average firms. They were just more efficient. Plain and simple.

High Growth firms are actually over 50% more profitable than average firms.

Growth and Profitability

That leaves the question of profitability. Does high growth come at the cost of operating profits? The answer surprised us. High growth firms are in fact over 50% more profitable than average firms. High growth and high profits—that's a killer combination.

In the next chapter, we'll zoom in and see how they are doing it.

Key Takeaways

- Increased spending on marketing and sales drives growth but was less efficient at the highest levels of investment.

- High growth, high value firms were growing nine times faster, were 50% more profitable, yet spent slightly less than average on marketing and sales.

eight:
high growth strategies that work

In chapter four we learned the importance of strategic growth in maximizing the value of a firm. But what kinds of strategies do high growth, high profit firms actually use?

Our research has revealed at least some of the answers. You may find a few of them counterintuitive at first, but they'll make more sense once you understand how they fit into the bigger picture.

Generalist or Specialist?

All professional services firms have to face this question: to what extent do you specialize? High growth firms show a marked tilt in the direction of specialization. Almost half of the firms we interviewed describe themselves as "very specialized." On a 0-10 scale of specialization, they rate themselves a 9 or 10.

High growth firms show a marked tilt in the direction of specialization.

The importance of specialization is very evident when firms describe their specific strategy. Strategies favored by high growth firms are consistent with a narrow focus and careful targeting. Average firms, however, are more likely to add new services and expend more energy on current clients. While this may sound like a safe approach, it dilutes a firm's focus and can slow its growth. New services require new skills and increased management attention.

Preferred Strategies

Favored By	Strategy Element
HIGH GROWTH	Narrowly Focused Target Client
	Use of Marketing Partnerships
	Offering Specialized Service
	Targeted Acquisitions
AVERAGE GROWTH	Go Deeper Within Current Client Base
	Add New Services
	Offering Technology/Service Mix

The Differentiation Difference

As we explained in chapter four, firms that differentiate themselves tend to command higher valuations. When a firm appears no different from its rivals, it's forced to compete on price alone. That said, differentiating a professional services firm can be a challenge. It's all too easy to fall back on, "We've got great people and superior technology, and we're devoted to our clients." Problem is, that's not newsworthy, and nobody wants to hear it. It's difficult to prove and sounds like marketing puffery.

So we dug into the issue of differentiation with great interest. We asked firms to describe their difference, then we rated how strong the differentiator really was. Was it understandable? Was it believable or supported by evidence? We found that high growth firms were almost three times more likely to have a very strong differentiator than firms that experienced average growth.

> High growth firms were almost 3x more likely to have a very strong differentiator.

A Strong Differentiator

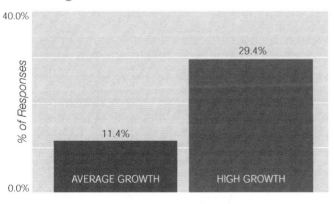

How a Firm Can Be Different

You may think it's impossible to differentiate your firm in today's homogenous professional services marketplace. Really, can one engineering firm or systems integrator be that different from another firm in the same industry?

Let's look at a few ways firms can differentiate themselves.

Differentiate by target audience. Suppose you run an accounting firm. You tell prospects that you offer business of all kinds, a wide range of services. Now suppose you're in charge of a firm that provides the same accounting services exclusively to ex-patriots. Which firm do you think has greater potential to gain awareness and stature among its target audience?

Differentiate by problem solved. Suppose you run an online marketing firm that helps many industries. Sounds like a whole host of firms out there. Now suppose you specialize in online marketing exclusively to the baby boom generation. You'd have a powerful difference to attract companies trying to reach that audience.

Differentiate by services offered. Suppose you run a technology firm that provides IT consulting services to a wide range of corporate and government clients. Okay. Now imagine your firm, instead, specializes in high risk, high reward IT projects exclusively for Fortune 500 clients using a small team of specialists and cutting edge technology. Within that niche, you'd be tough to beat.

Differentiate by business model. Suppose that most firms in your industry bill by the hour for services provided. What if your firm went a different direction and offered fixed priced, project based pricing. Again, you would have a clear difference.

Each of these examples come from real firms that sacrificed broad appeal to focus on and capture a specific market. You can do it too. How? Begin by looking at what you already do exceptionally well, then chip away at everything else. Assuming what's left is big enough to sustain your firm's growth, focus your message like a laser on that competitive advantage.

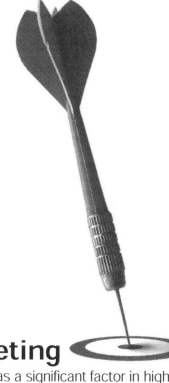

Client Targeting

Clearly, differentiation was a significant factor in high growth potential. What about narrowly targeting customer segments? Was that also an advantage? When we asked CEOs to describe their target client, those in the high growth group were over three times more likely to provide a very detailed and specific answer.

This makes sense, when you think about it. By narrowly defining their audience, a firm can put more resources toward converting them into clients. That results in greater efficiency and profitability—exactly the pattern we see in our research.

> By narrowly defining their audience, a firm can put more resources toward converting them into clients.

Know Your Potential Client

As experienced professionals, we know our target market and their needs pretty well. Or do we? Some firms were putting a lot of effort into surveying their target market and trying to understand their needs and priorities. But is ongoing client research worth it? We divided firms into three categories:

- Those who conduct formal target market research on a frequent basis (at least quarterly)

- Those who conduct research occasionally

- Those who don't do any research

The clarity and strength of the results surprised us.

Research and Results

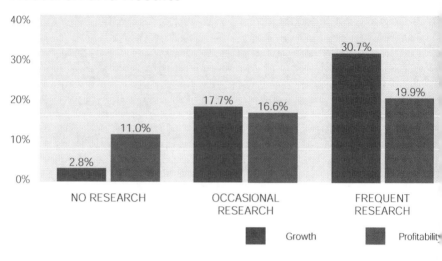

As you can see in the chart, systematic research into potential client needs and priorities results in higher growth and profits. The more you know, the more you grow. Apparently, understanding your potential clients' needs pays off in a very direct fashion. How? Well, a firm that understands its target markets' changing needs and priorities is better prepared to anticipate and meet them. That's a compelling advantage.

Systematic research into potential client needs and priorities results in higher growth and profits.

How to Conduct Target Client Research

There is more to target client research than client satisfaction surveys. The type of research that provides actionable insights is systematic and structured. It requires spending time talking, typically by phone, to actual or potential customers in your target audience.

As you develop your list of questions, think about what knowledge will make you more relevant to your potential clients: current and emerging business issues, trends, industry challenges—anything that might help you understand your target group and anticipate their needs. If you don't have the experience or time, consider hiring an outside firm. When we've done this kind of research for our clients, we routinely discover issues of interest to their clients and points of view they have never considered.

The research has a number of ancillary benefits, as well. You can use it as an enticement to get in front of key prospects. And you can communicate your findings in articles, public speaking and blog entries (maybe even a book!). It can add a new dimension to your marketing program.

Marketing Tools

We were also interested in finding out which marketing approaches high growth, high value firms favor. After asking CEOs to rate various marketing approaches, we then compared responses from high growth firms to average firms. We were immediately struck by how the tools favored by high growth firms lend themselves to a targeted strategy.

The tools favored by high growth firms lend themselves to a targeted strategy.

Preferred Marketing Tools

Average Growth	High Growth
Formal Distributorships	Partnering
Conferences and Trade Shows	Website
Networking	Referrals
Cold Calls	Outside Experts and Consultants
Print Advertising	Sales Training for Non-Sales Staff
Email	Personal Visits to Prospects
Direct Mail/Postal	

Top Management Focus

Where should a firm's top management focus their attention? What barriers are they trying to overcome?

When we asked CEOs to identify barriers to their firm's growth, we received very different responses from the two groups of firms. Average growth CEOs focused on the economy and competition—not too surprisingly, given recent economic turmoil. In contrast, their high growth counterparts were focusing on marketing and business development, financing growth and finding the right people. That says a lot!

A Better Way

So now we've come full circle. We've discovered that there are indeed better ways to build a professional services firm. There is a group of clever firms that grow faster, are more profitable and command a higher premium in the marketplace. They employ strategies that are sometimes counterintuitive and favor certain practices over others.

We've also learned that no single technique or strategy is "the answer." High growth and high value are built incrementally, one step at a time. A better strategy improves client targeting. Better targeting improves marketing efficiency. Improved efficiency speeds growth. Gradually, the upward spiral builds momentum.

In the next chapter, we're going to turn our attention to the practical challenge of implementing a high growth, high value strategy. Let's start by taking a trip to the shopping mall.

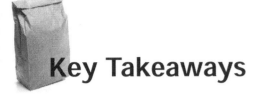

Key Takeaways

¬ High growth firms tend to specialize and are much more likely to have strong, easy-to-understand differentiators.

¬ High growth firms have carefully targeted clients and understand them well.

¬ Firms that frequently and systematically research target client needs and priorities are often more profitable and grow faster.

¬ Marketing tools and management focus support these strategies.

nine:
you are here

Have you ever walked into an unfamiliar shopping mall or airport and been utterly confused? Where am I? Where do I go? How do I get there?

Then you see that helpful map—the one with the arrow that says "You are here." Think of this chapter as your map—a guide to take you from "here" to where you want to go.

What It Takes to Succeed—An Overview

If you've gotten this far, you probably want to know how you can apply this book's lessons to your own firm. It's time to pull all of our research findings together into a coordinated plan of attack: a practical plan for building a high growth, high value firm.

We'll begin by taking a high-level, birds-eye view of our approach. For your professional services firm to be successful you've got to have three key areas covered: strategy, people and operations.

Strategy is the key to high growth and a premium valuation.

Strategy

Strategy is the key to high growth and a premium valuation. Get the strategy right and the rest is easier. What goes into a good strategy?

- ○ Understand and anticipate your client's needs.

- ○ Make sure your services solve key business problems.

- ○ Deliver superior value.

- ○ Have a well-thought-out strategy to differentiate your firm and position it in the marketplace.

If you can accomplish these things, then getting new business becomes a lot simpler. In our experience, firms with a successful strategy are able to maintain a steady flow of the "right kind" of new clients.

People

In the professional services, people are the product. This makes hiring the right individuals for the right roles crucial to a firm's success. And as most firm executives know from hard-won experience, finding and retaining talent can be devilishly difficult. You'll know you are successful in this area when you are able to attract and keep the high-quality new hires you need to maintain sustainable growth.

Operations

Can you reliably and cost-effectively deliver on what you promise? Firms that can confidently answer "yes" to this question tend to have profitable, satisfied clients— clients that make valuable referrals. These clients become an engine of sustainable growth and contribute to premium valuations. You'll know you are successful if you've got a smooth process, a healthy bottom line and an accumulation of loyal, referring clients.

Which area is most important? Each one is essential to building a healthy, growing firm. As we'll explain in the next chapter, however, your best bet is to get your strategy right first, then build from there.

So Where Are You?

Understanding where your firm stands in each of
these critical areas is not as easy as it sounds. Most of
us are very good at deceiving ourselves. For instance,
we want to have a strong competitive advantage, so
we talk ourselves into believing that we have one.
(This could be a big reason why high growth firms use
outside marketing resources more often—they help
firms remain unbiased in their self-assessments.) If
you want to know where you are, however, you have
to try to be objective and willing to acknowledge
your weaknesses.

> If you want to know where you are,
> you have to be objective and willing to
> acknowledge your weaknesses.

To get you started, we've created a marketing self-
assessment instrument*—a series of questions to ask
yourself and your team. Your team's answers will help
you understand where your firm stands today.

Try to answer each of the following questions honestly.
The more people in your firm who participate, the
better your data will be.

*A convenient version of this instrument is available for download at
www.spiralingupbook.com/resources.

Strategy

Strategic Growth

To grow, your firm needs an understandable and easily communicated strategy.

- ○ What is the market and need for your service?

- ○ Is it a healthy and growing segment?

- ○ Why will you succeed where other firms do not?

- ○ What will success look like for your firm?

- ○ Can you describe your strategy clearly and succinctly?

Well Understood Target Group

You must have a clearly defined and well understood target market.

- ○ Have you analyzed your current clients to determine how to define your best target group?

- ○ Do you understand their problems, concerns, fears, hopes and daily reality?

- ○ Can you get specific?

- ○ Do you conduct regular research on your clients and/or their industry to anticipate needs and uncover trends?

- Can you identify the best channels to communicate to your target market?

- Does your firm have credibility with your target audience?

- Have they heard of your firm?

Compelling Value Proposition

You must be able to solve important client problems in a way that delivers a significant economic impact or makes their life much easier.

- Does your service produce a direct economic benefit for clients? Can you prove it?

- Will it clearly make their life easier? Can you prove it?

- Does your service address an issue that potential clients really care about?

- Can you communicate the value you bring in a clear and compelling way?

Clear Differentiator

You should be different from your potential competitors in a way that is understandable, meaningful and believable to prospective clients.

- Can you describe your firm in a way that other firms cannot?

- How are you different?

- Can you prove it?

- Do potential clients really care?

- Do your competitors acknowledge the difference?

People

Talented, Well Matched People

You must have a sufficient supply of talented people who are well matched to their jobs and can connect with clients.

- Do you have enough people with the right technical skills and credentials?

- Are their personalities and people skills a good fit with your target clients?

- Do they have the right business values and appropriate attitude?

- Can you easily hire more people as your needs grow?

- Do your people represent your brand well?

- Can all your people clearly and succinctly describe what you do, who you do it for, and why you are different?

Strong Middle Management

You must have a strong middle management team that can effectively guide the day-to-day functioning of the firm.

- Do you have a middle management team in place?

- Can they run day-to-day operations without help from top management?

- Is there a practical plan in place to build the ranks as the firm grows?

- Do middle managers embrace your firm's strategy?

- Do they reflect well on the brand?

Operations

Deliver on Your Brand Promise

You must be able to deliver on the promise that you explicitly and implicitly make to your clients.

- Do your clients believe you deliver what you promise?

- Does your staff believe you do what you promise for your clients?

- Do clients consistently refer your firm to their friends and colleagues?

- What is your reputation in the marketplace?

- What do your competitors say about your firm?

Believable Growth Projections

You must have the systems in place to make believable, fact-based projections.

- Are your projections based on verifiable facts and trends?

- Are your projections historically accurate?

- Can you document the relationship between marketing spending and new business development?

- Do you have the ability to accelerate or decelerate business growth?

- Is your growth scalable?

Solid, Believable Financial Results

You must have financial results that are both believable and demonstrate the ability to generate acceptable returns.

- ○ Is your growth rate superior to competitors?

- ○ Are your earnings comparable or superior to competitors?

- ○ Are your accounting assumptions considered conservative?

- ○ Are financials up-to-date and produced on a regular and timely basis?

- ○ Can you accurately predict future financial performance?

Once you have completed this exercise, compare your answers with those of others in your firm. Discuss the inevitable differences and try to form a consensus. If you can't reach consensus, go with the more pessimistic assessment. (In our experience, it's probably more accurate. Sorry.)

Now that you have a baseline understanding of your firm, it's time to make some changes. It's time to put your firm on an upward spiral.

Key Takeaways

¬ Growing a successful professional services firm takes a solid strategy, the right people and strong operations.

¬ Failure in any of these areas will limit your growth potential.

¬ Use our self-assessment instrument. Be honest with yourself.

ten:

starting your upward spiral

If your firm is like most, you have a lot of work to do. You may find the number of areas that need attention to be extensive, even overwhelming. We understand. Running a professional services firm is already a full-time job, and it may be hard to imagine how you're going to transform your firm into a high-performing superstar.

Don't let the magnitude of the challenge stop you in your tracks. The spiraling up process is incremental, and organizational change takes time, even in the best of circumstances. We're ending this book with a process to get you started. This process should save you a lot of time and wasted effort, and it will help you take real steps toward meaningful, progressive change.

Strategy First

In the previous chapter, we identified three key marketing areas – strategy, people and operations – that are essential to a firm's long-term success. But that doesn't mean you should address these issues in just any order.

If you think about it, you can't really refine your operations to deliver on your brand promise until you know what that promise is. Similarly, what makes a person right for a firm depends on what kind of service you are planning to deliver. And you can't refine your services until you've defined your target clients. Bottom line? Before you do anything else, get your strategy right.

First you have to get your strategy right. |

Revolutionary or Evolutionary?

How much change can you afford to make? Should you start with a clean slate?

If we assume that you have an established firm with real clients and a few years of history, we'd recommend that you build on what you have already. We've seen many firms formulate exciting new strategies and successes using an evolutionary approach. Think of it as the "soft reboot" that starts your firm on its upward spiral.

Start Here

Do Your Homework

First, make sure you have a reasonably accurate understanding of your firm's marketing leverage. The best way to do this yourself is to perform an honest assessment of your company using the instrument introduced in chapter nine.

Do the Research

Begin learning everything you can about your markets and your clients. Find out which markets are likely to grow and thrive. You can get some of this information from industry associations and market research firms, but most firms get the most relevant information by conducting custom research into their target audience. This market research will help you understand the environment you are competing in. Next, turn your focus on your clients. Figure out which types of clients you want to grow and which ones to avoid. Then talk to them. If you can afford it, have a third-party resource conduct phone interviews—you'll get more honest feedback. Your findings will help you assess how you are perceived in the marketplace. Finally, try to understand what you do well already and where you need to improve.

You must understand how you are perceived in the marketplace.

> If it feels comfortable, its not likely to be a great strategy.

Invest in Strategy

Put time and resources into understanding where your real opportunities lie. Resist the powerful temptation to try to be everything to everyone—it doesn't really make getting new business easier. In fact, business development is more difficult because you have more competition. Avoid doing what's comfortable—chances are, your peers are doing it, too. If it feels completely comfortable, it's not likely to be a great strategy. When you believe you have a winning strategy, do what it takes to embrace it. Write it down, discuss it and get the whole team onboard.

> Nothing will change until you start to do things differently.

Make Real Changes

Nothing will change until you start to do things differently. Sometimes change just needs a catalyst to catch on. Redesign your website, revise your marketing materials, hire different people, or revise your processes. No strategy, however clever or well thought out, will have an impact unless it's implemented. This can take courage and money. But few firms ever regret taking that step.

We hope you will take the lessons in this book to heart. They are based on real-world data gleaned from some of the nation's most successful professional services firms. The path we've described in this final chapter is just the beginning of your journey—a remarkable course that could lead your firm to new levels of growth and profitability. The process of understanding your audience, adjusting to changing conditions, generating new business and delivering on your brand promise never ends. But if your firm can adopt a culture of ongoing, incremental improvement, it will become, over time, a formidable contender. May your spiral up be an inspiration for us all!

Key Takeaways

- ¬ Begin by getting your strategy right.

- ¬ Base your strategy on an objective understanding of your firm's strengths and your target audience.

- ¬ Your strategy is useless unless you implement it.

additional resources

The goal of this section is to give you access to some key resources that we have found helpful in shaping our thinking and growing our business. We are deliberately trying to be selective rather than comprehensive.

In the **Primary Research Studies** we review the four original studies that form the basis of the book. These resources are available free on our website at www.hingemarketing.com/library. You'll also find a broad selection of articles, white papers, podcasts and videos on strategy, branding and marketing your professional service firm.

We also share a few selected blogs in **Branding and Marketing Blogs** that we find most useful and relevant for ourselves and our clients. These are applicable across all professional services segments.

Finally, we share selected blogs and helpful trade and professional associations that are relevant to specific types of firms in the **Industry Verticals** section. Don't be shy about exploring what other professional services industries are up to.

If you know of a very useful resource that we haven't included, please contact us at 703.391.8870 or at info@hingemarketing.com. Enjoy!

Primary Research Studies

Defying Gravity This original study of 100 professional services firms between $1 million and $1 billion in annual revenue focuses on strategy and marketing. We identified high growth companies across all segments and documented what those high growth companies do differently. This research is covered in chapters 2 and 3.

Top Dollar We examine firms that achieve premium valuations. Hinge interviewed acquirers of companies and valuation experts to determine the specific factors that drive extremely high multiples ("the Google effect") and what strategic moves CEOs can make to put their firm in the same category. This research is covered in chapter 4.

Professional Services: How Buyers Buy For this study, we conducted in-depth interviews with private and public sector professional service buyers. We uncover the full life-cycle of an engagement, including firm selection, expanding the relationship, factors driving referrals, and ending the relationship. This research is covered in chapters 5 and 6.

The High Growth Professional Services Firm The high growth firms in this study grew 9x faster and were 50% more profitable than their average growth peers. Yet they spent less than average on marketing and sales. We explore what high growth firms do differently from their average growth peers and we uncover what characteristics contribute to their success. This research is covered in chapters 7 and 8.

Branding and Marketing Blogs

Brian Solis, @BrianSolis
www.briansolis.com

Ian Brodie
www.ianbrodie.com

Suzanne Lowe, Expertise Marketing
www.expertisemarketing.com

David Maister, Professional Business Professional Life
www.davidmaister.com/blog (note: David is retired but his blog archives are timeless.)

Chris Brogan
www.chrisbrogan.com

Andrew Sobel, The Business of Relationships
www.andrewsobel.com/blog

Charles H. Green, Trust Matters
www.trustedadvisor.com/trustmatters

Jay Baer, Convince and Convert
www.convinceandconvert.com/

Sonja Jefferson, Valuable Content
www.sonjajefferson.co.uk/

Marketing Experiments
www.marketingexperiments.com

RainMaker Blog
www.raintodayblog.com

Jeremy Victor, B2B Bloggers
www.b2bbloggers.com

Proteus Marketing
www.proteusb2b.com/b2b-marketing-blog/

Brand Flakes for Breakfast
www.brandflakesforbreakfast.com/

Kipp Bodnar, Social Media B2B
www.socialmediab2b.com

Christine "CK" Kerley, CK's B2B Blog
www.ck-blog.com

Government Contracting Associations and Blogs

Small and Emerging Contractors Advisory Forum
www.secaf.org/

Armed Forces Communications and Electronics
www.afcea.org/

Aronson Blogs
www.aronsonblogs.com

govloop
www.govloop.com

Judy Bradt, Sell2USGOV
www.sell2usgov.blogspot.com/

Washington Technology
www.washingtontechnology.com/blogs

Technology Associations and Blogs

Information Technology Services Marketing
Association *www.itsma.com/*

Northern Virginia Technology Council
www.nvtc.org/index.php

TechAmerica
www.TechAmerica.org/

Paul Dunay, Buzz Marketing for Technology
www.pauldunay.com

Christopher Koch, B2B Marketing Blog
www.christopherakoch.com/

Government Computer News
www.gcn.com/blogs/tech-blog/list/blog-list.aspx

Tech Republic
www.blogs.techrepublic.com

A/E/C Associations and Blogs

American Institute of Architects
www.aia.org/

American Society of Engineering Management
https://www.netforumondemand.com/eweb/
StartPage.aspx?Site=asem&WebCode=HomePage&Fr
omSearchControl=Yes

American Society of Civil Engineers
www.asce.org/

Society for Marketing of Professional Services
www.smps.org/

Associated Builders & Contractors
www.abc.org/

Commercial Real Estate Women (CREW)
www.crewnetwork.org/

American Council of Engineering Companies of
Metropolitan Washington *www.acecmw.org/*

NAIOP Research Foundation
www.naiop.org/foundation/home.cfm

Matt Handal, Help Everybody Everyday
www.helpeverybodyeveryday.com/

Ed Hannan, PSMJ Research
www.psmj.blogspot.com/

Tim Klabunde, Cofebuz
www.cofebuz.com/

ZweigWhite, The Board Room
www.zweigwhite.blogspot.com/

Ford Harding, Harding & Company
www.hardingco.com/blog/

Construction Law North Carolina
www.constructionlawNC.com/

PE Community
http://community.nspe.org/blogs/

Management Consulting Associations and Blogs

Association of Management Consulting Firms
www.amcf.org

Institute of Management Consultants USA
www.imcusa.com

Society of Human Resource Management
www.shrm.org

Tom Peters, Tom Peters!
www.tompeters.com

Michael McLaughlin, Guerilla Consulting
www.guerillaconsulting.typepad.com

Alan Weiss, Contrarian Consulting
www.contrarianconsulting.com

Accounting & Finance Services Associations and Blogs

Association for Accounting Marketing
www.accountingmarketing.org

American Institute of CPAs
www.aicpa.org

The Middle Market Investment Banking Association
www.mmiba.com/

Investment Management of Consultants Associations
www.IMCA.org

Michelle Golden, Golden Practices Blog
www.goldenmarketing.typepad.com

re: The Auditors
www.retheauditors.com/

CPA Trendlines
www.cpatrendlines.com/

Craig Weeks, Accounting Practice Business
Development *www.acctbizblog.com*

Dennis Howlett, AccMan
www.accmanpro.com

Legal Associations and Blogs

Legal Marketing Association
www.legalmarketing.org

Kevin O'Keefe, Real Lawyers Have Blogs
www.kevin.lexblog.com/

Eric Goldman, Technology & Marketing Law Blog
www.blog.ericgoldman.org/

Larry Bodine, Law Marketing Blog
www.larrybodine.com/blog

Gerry Riskin, Amazing Firms, Amazing Practices
www.gerryriskin.com

about the team

Any project of this magnitude has a team behind it. Meet the Hinge team, including the authors and key project leaders.

Lee W. Frederiksen, Ph.D. : Author

Lee is Managing Partner at Hinge, a premier professional services branding and marketing firm. He brings over 30 years of marketing experience to the firm's clients. Lee is a former tenured professor of psychology at Virginia Tech, author of numerous books and articles, and a successful entrepreneur. He's started and run three high-growth companies, including an $80 million runaway success. Lee has worked with many global brands, including American Express, Time Life, Capital One, Monster.com and Yahoo! He led the research studies that form the basis of the book.

 lwf@hingemarketing.com

 www.linkedin.com/in/leefrederiksen

Aaron E. Taylor : Author

Aaron is a founding partner at Hinge. In his almost 20 years in the industry, he has been an award-winning designer, editor, strategist and writer. Over his career, he's conceived and implemented engaging brand strategies for many professional services firms. Aaron has been published widely in local, regional and national business publications and industry magazines.

 aaron@hingemarketing.com

 www.linkedin.com/in/aarontaylorva

Sylvia Montgomery : Marketing Program

From initial creative discussions to reviewer outreach, production and the overall marketing of Spiraling Up, Sylvia rules the marketing plan. As a seasoned marketing executive with origins in graphic design, Sylvia has led marketing teams at several technology and consulting firms—from start-ups to Fortune 500 firms. Sylvia is a published author and speaker; previously she has served as an adjunct professor at both Trinity College and the George Washington University. At Hinge, Sylvia leads the Outsourced Marketing practice, engaging with clients on a daily basis and drives Hinge's own marketing initiatives.

 sylvia@hingemarketing.com

 @brandstrong

 www.linkedin.com/in/sylviamontgomery

Candace Frederiksen :
Executive Interviews

Every journey begins with a single step and every
research study begins with a phone call. So did
this book. The executives in our research receive a
call from Candace. A seasoned entrepreneur with
over 20 years of product development, production
and campaign management experience, Candace
conducts our in-depth interviews with senior
executives. Over the course of her career, she has
managed hundreds of research and marketing
campaigns. At Hinge, she manages client services,
project management resources and day-to-day
client relations.

 candace@hingemarketing.com

 www.linkedin.com/in/candacefrederiksen

about hinge

Hinge is a national branding and marketing firm for the professional services industry, including Architecture, Engineering and Construction (A/E/C), Technology, Management Consulting, Accounting and Finance, and Government Contracting. Hinge services include Client Research, Brand Strategy Development, Graphic Design & Other Creative Services, Content Development, Website Development, Online Video Production, and Outsourced Marketing Services. For more information on Hinge, visit www.hingemarketing.com.

For free branding and marketing strategies for your professional service, follow us on Twitter and subscribe to our blog.

 @HingeMarketing

 www.hingemarketing.com/blog

about hinge research institute

At Hinge, research is more than skin deep. It helps define who we are, how we help our clients and guides how we grow our firm. We also believe in sharing our knowledge, not only with our clients but also with the broader professional services community. This commitment has led to the establishment of Hinge Research Institute. The Institute is committed to conducting innovative research on professional services firms and their respective clients. We are also committed to sharing that knowledge through research studies, webinars, executive roundtables, whitepapers, articles and books. Please visit us at www.hingeresearch.com to see additional white papers, pod casts and research reports.

Breinigsville, PA USA
30 January 2011
254403BV00004BB/2/P